THIS BOOK BELONGS TO

FUN MIKE PRESS © All rights reserved.
No part of this publication may be reproduced, distributed, or transmitted
In any form or by any means, including photocopying, recording,
Without the prior written permission of the publisher.

COLOR TEST PAGE

Find the correct shadow

Find the correct shadow

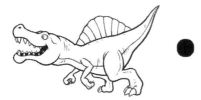 

Made in the USA
Columbia, SC
19 February 2022

56467307R00037